Guaranteed
SUCCESS
When You
Never Give Up

Guaranteed
SUCCESS
When You
Never Give Up

PERCY "MASTER P" MILLER

The Wealthy Son

www.urbanbooks.net

Urban Books
1199 Straight Path
West Babylon, NY 11704

ISBN-13: 978-1-60162-112-2
ISBN-10: 1-60162-112-4

Hardcover September 2007
Printed in the United States of America

10 9 8 7 6 5 4 3 2 1

Submit Wholesale Orders to:
Kensington Publishing Corp.
C/O Penguin Group (USA) Inc.
Attention: Order Processing
405 Murray Hill Parkway
East Rutherford, NJ 07073-2316
Phone: 1-800-526-0275
Fax: 1-800-227-9604

TABLE OF CONTENTS

INTRODUCTION

Everyday challenges and social pressures can make a fulfilling, successful life of purpose seem impossible to attain. That's why I wrote this book. I believe it's my responsibility to share my life's journey from emptiness to fulfillment, poverty to prosperity, lack to purpose, and failure to success. My goal is to make you aware that success is indeed attainable in all aspects of *your* life.

Anything is possible if you can first perceive it (*see it manifested in your own mind*), then believe it (*have absolute faith*), and finally, refuse to give up until you achieve it (*actively pursue your goal every day*).

Success is a journey, not a destination.

Success is not an end in itself; it's not a one-time event. And it's definitely not just about having *things* (money, possessions, recognition, and status). To live a *successful life*, a person must achieve a series of *progressive* life goals. True success contributes to the development of a person as a whole: spiritually, mentally, emotionally, physically, and financially. Ideally, the growth of success is continuous and gradual, passing from one temporary stage of life into the next. It's ongoing, never ceasing, always progressing.

Success takes time; it doesn't happen overnight. It's a process; it's about developing yourself, staying focused, setting goals that benefit others (consequently benefiting you), engaging yourself effectively to achieve the results *you* desire from your goals, overcoming obstacles, getting back up when life knocks you down, standing for something so that you don't fall for anything, finding your way back when you get off track, and *never giving up* . . . that's success!

During my life's journey I've discovered that God has blessed each of us with unique abilities, also known as talents. It is the responsibility of each individual to decide *what to do* with those talents and *how to share* them. It's not what you have or how much you have, but *what you do with what you have* that determines your success or lack of it.

It all starts with knowing who you *truly* are—and what better way to find out than by asking through prayer to the One who created you. The more you get to know *your* Creator, the more you realize who *you* are, what you are really capable of, and what your unique and true purpose is for being here on this earth at this present time. Don't waste another day; live every single day with purpose! Realize there's no limit to the abundance of potential within you; it's waiting to be awakened by your passion so that you can successfully live your life for an *everlasting* purpose.

You have the ability to change *any* area of your life. If you're not getting the results you want in some part of your life, it makes sense that you'll have to do something different to get different results. After all, your past decisions and actions (or lack thereof) have led you to where you are today. The choices you make or *don't* make today determine your success or lack of it tomorrow.

Start guaranteeing your success right now by writing down your answers to the vitally important questions included throughout the following chapters. This is *your* book; interact with it and write in it—your thoughts, your ideas, your questions, your answers, your revelations, and anything else your heart desires! Don't waste your time and energy just *reading* this book; take the time to answer the questions *truthfully*, and you will be guaranteeing your own success. The questions included in each chapter were written specifically for *you*. Answer them as you go along and grow with me!

CHAPTER ONE

WHAT IS THE FIRST KEY TO SUCCESS?

The first key to success is *awareness*. Before making any life-altering changes, you must become completely aware of your individual circumstances. Once you have established awareness of your current situation, you will be able to gain the necessary *knowledge* to make effective decisions that will bring about the results you desire.

You can start with where you are in your life right at this moment. Take an honest look at yourself and your life. Now ask yourself, "Is this what I want for my life? Where will I be in ten years if I continue to live the way I do right now? Where do I want to be ten years from now? What steps do I need to take to accomplish that goal?"

These are serious questions. After all, you only

have one life to live. Why not live it to the fullest and with purpose?

I remember asking myself those questions when I was sixteen years old. I was sitting on the park bench, hanging out with the other kids, as we regularly did. We were taking turns pointing out the nice cars that drove by and then claiming them as "ours" by saying something like, "That's my car!" The kids pointed mostly at the Cadillacs and the flashy Oldsmobile Cutlasses. If we happened to see a Mercedes-Benz (which was rare in our neighborhood), no one dared or even bothered to point at it and claim it as theirs; it just seemed so far out of reach.

On this particular day, we saw a Mercedes-Benz. I realized that was the car I wanted. I knew that the man who was driving was an entrepreneur, a legitimate businessman selling life insurance to the people in the ghetto. And when I told my friends that I wanted "that car right there," one of my friends said, "You'll never be able to afford a car like that!" And I responded, "Yes I will! As a matter of fact, I'll have two of them!"

When I went back to my house, I had to face the harsh reality. We had a house full of people and an empty refrigerator. I was so hungry that my stomach was literally cramping. In that moment, I said to myself, "I can't live like this . . . I need to figure out a way to help feed myself and my family." So I started visualizing myself in that Mercedes-Benz. I could see myself driving it through my neighborhood, bringing my grandmother to and from the grocery store, being able to buy as much food as we saw fit.

Sure enough, during my senior year of high school, I started my first real entrepreneurial business. I took the money that I had saved throughout the years from the odd jobs that I did (mowing lawns, carrying groceries, assisting elderly, running errands, etc.) and invested it into the newest, hottest selling item in that day: cell phones. Remember when cell phones were first manufactured and they were gigantic and heavy—like they were straight out of *The Flintstones?* Well, I purchased these cell phones from a major cell phone company at wholesale price and then sold them below the retail price. I even hand-delivered them when I was selling to my high-profile clients—mostly professional football players who played for the New Orleans Saints.

Now I was able to help buy groceries, pay rent, and pay some of the house bills. No one in my family could find a job at the time. I couldn't find one either, so I created my own. I was working as an entrepreneur, not an employee. I learned that no matter what your present circumstances look like, you can take yourself wherever you want to go if you can visualize a brighter future through the eyes of faith. If you're *just surviving*, you don't have to stay there; you can visualize a *purposeful* future and then take yourself there one step at a time.

The diagram below illustrates the three main stages in life, from the "just surviving" **Caterpillar Stage** to the "purposeful" **Butterfly Stage**.

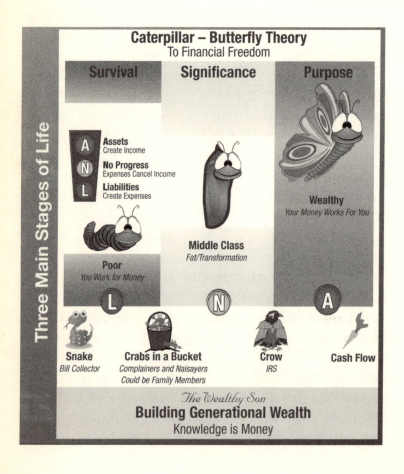

What stage do you think you're most likely in right now ("Caterpillar," "Cocoon," or "Butterfly")? What makes you think so? Are you satisfied with being in that stage? Why or why not?

_____

_____

_____

_____

_____

_____

_____

_____

_____

_____

_____

_____

_____

Most people find themselves in what I call the **Caterpillar Stage** of life. This is when a person has no awareness of his or her individual maximum potential. This person has no knowledge of the unique purpose for his or her life. He or she is settling for mediocrity, living below the minimum standards of a quality life, and barely getting by due to tremendous lack—whether it's a lack of spiritual knowledge, lack of academic or financial education, lack of vocational training, lack of self-confidence, lack of self-discipline, lack of self-motivation, lack of guidance, or lack of direction.

They simply continue to live day-to-day, struggling in the "Survival Stage" of life without any forward progress. They live every day without the *awareness* of their maximum potential and without the *knowledge* of their true purpose.

> *Success comes in levels;*
> *it's not a once in a lifetime event.*

Now, some people outgrow the **Caterpillar Stage** and mature into what I call the **Cocoon Stage**. This is the "Transformational Stage" where someone makes a conscious decision to position himself or herself in his or her own "Cocoon," and the transformation from the "Caterpillar" to the "Butterfly" begins to take place. They have come to the realization that life has more to offer than just struggling in the "Survival Stage."

As my grandmother would put it, this happens when someone is "sick and tired of being sick and tired." They realize they have not yet discovered their maximum potential and that their true purpose does in fact exist. This is also what I consider the "Significant Stage" of a person's life because they *thrive* in this stage, staying focused on their goals as they seek to discover their true purpose in life.

Success is achieved in progressive installments.

Then there are those who actually prosper in life, in what I call the **Butterfly Stage**. Through faithful dedication to living a life of excellence *with purpose*, they finally develop by complete "metamorphosis." This critical process of development takes place inside the "Cocoon" where they persevered through their "Transformational Stage" as they exercised their power to choose.

They chose to make a lifetime commitment to invest in themselves. They chose to empower themselves with spiritual knowledge, financial or academic education, vocational training, self-discipline, self-motivation, guidance, and direction.

People can enter the **Cocoon Stage** at any age, and the length of time a person spends in this stage varies—depending on the individual's unique circumstances and attitudes about life. Looking back, I believe that my initial entrance into the **Cocoon Stage** happened as I was graduating from high school. My whole life, I had heard people *complaining* about how hard life is (complaints were usually financially related), *comparing* themselves with others in a negative way (mostly nonsense gossip of what so-and-so has and what so-and-so is doing), and *making countless excuses* for why it was impossible to be "successful."

I was so tired of the many years of hearing the complaining, the comparing, and the countless excuses that never ended. I wanted to *do something* about my life, and I realized I needed to further my education and go to college. So my goal was to go to a university in Louisiana or Texas. Not one of my friends shared this goal. And most of the people around me said that I wouldn't be able to survive in a university because I'm black and from the ghetto. They said I didn't belong in college, especially not a university. I disagreed. I attended the University of Houston on an athletic scholarship and majored in Business Communications.

If you were to go into a "Transformational Cocoon," what would it look like? What would you do in that stage? How would you invest in yourself?

_____

_____

_____

_____

_____

_____

_____

_____

The people who spend time in the "Transformational Cocoon," bettering themselves, learning, and gaining knowledge and awareness become successful in every noteworthy area of their lives. They make a decision to invest in themselves and focus on their strengths. Eventually, they unveil their true purpose and enter into the "Butterfly Stage."

If you had to say right now what your life's purpose is, what would it be? What would it feel like to emerge as the "Butterfly"? What would your life look like in that stage?

_____

_____

_____

_____

_____

_____

_____

_____

_____

Some people assume the **Butterfly Stage** is all about money. Don't make that mistake. There's a common misconception that when a person acquires more money, more happiness is an automatic result. Throughout my life, I've heard people say _"I'll be so happy when I make more money,"_ or _"I'll be happy when I pay off my bills,"_ or _"Who said money can't buy happiness? I sure wouldn't mind trying!"_ or _"If I had more money, I wouldn't_ *have these problems!"* It's delusional to surrender that kind of power to money when you have that power within yourself.

Money is only a tool.

Too many people fail to realize that money is just a *tool*. Every person has the opportunity to create income. And each person possesses his or her own individual right to use money to his or her advantage or *misuse* it to his or her disadvantage. You can use money to provide the type of lifestyle (comfort, luxury, extravagance, etc.) and physical environment (better neighborhood, schooling, socializing, recreation, etc.) that you desire. However, money can only *add* to or *subtract* from your happiness, depending on *how* you use it or abuse it.

There are a lot of financially successful people out there who are not successfully happy. I've met plenty of multimillionaires who are not happy, whether it's because their health is deteriorating, their marriage is failing or is a scam, or their family members (and friends, if they have any) are plagued by deceit and envy. In some cases, they're not completely happy because they feel like there's something missing in their lives. It reminds me of The Notorious B.I.G.'s song called "Mo' money, Mo' problems"—for many folks, this is true!

It's one of life's biggest mistakes to live for money. Why live for money? When you die, you can't take it with you! (Have you ever seen a U-Haul in a funeral procession?) Of course, it helps to have money. We all know that money is essential for survival; you need it because you have to buy food, put clothes on your back, and put a roof over your head. That's a part of life. And of course, who wants to just "survive" in life when there is so much more? However, having money alone does not make you happy, nor does it make you a success.

True success is a byproduct of happiness. That means success is an inevitable result of being happy. Anybody can make money, but true happiness comes from living a purposeful life.

How did you do? Did you increase your SELF-AWARENESS by answering the questions as you read this chapter?

I can't stress enough how vitally important it is for you to answer every single question in this book. You will be exposed to new information throughout each chapter, which may influence your answers. Continue to answer the questions as you go along because as you read further into this book, your answers may change. It's important for you to know why they're changing.

Your answers and revelations, in total, will give

you the exact guidance and direction that you need to guarantee your future successes. If you're not answering the questions, you're limiting the level of success that you can achieve! The FIRST KEY to SUCCESS is AWARENESS!

My thoughts, my ideas, my questions, my answers, my affirmations, and my revelations for *Chapter 1: What is the FIRST KEY to SUCCESS?*

_____

_____

_____

_____

_____

_____

_____

_____

_____

_____

_____

_____

_____

_____

_____

_____

_____

_____

_____

_____

_____

_____

CHAPTER TWO

WHAT IS SUCCESS?

What does it mean to be successful? What does success mean to you? Why is it so important to people? What does it take to be successful?

Success is defined as: *the gaining of something desired, planned, or attempted; the gaining of fame and prosperity and/or the extent of such gain; an expected result or outcome.* That's the **standard** definition for success, but you have to personally define it for yourself.

There are different aspects of success. Here are the *Four Main Categories for Success:*

- SPIRITUAL

- PERSONAL

- BUSINESS

- FINANCIAL

Looking at yourself right now, do you consider yourself a "success"? Why or why not?

_____

_____

_____

_____

_____

_____

_____

Knowledge and **understanding** are essential to attracting success. You gain a sense of direction as you seek out knowledge and understanding in the area you want to be successful in. This applies to any desire that you may have. Wherever you desire to be successful in your life, you must first understand it and arm yourself with knowledge. It is *your* responsibility to educate yourself!

Success is important to everyone in one way or another. I believe it's because the desire for success has been built in us. We have a natural desire to succeed in the things that we put our hands on. Our desires, motives, and reasons for success may differ, but we *all* want it.

Success is available to every one of us.

I've come to believe that God created us in this way: He gave each of us the ability to succeed. That's why we crave success—it's our human instinct, and that's why we feel such satisfaction when we achieve *any* type of success. As we accomplish success, we fulfill a void in us. And with every success, we grow and mature, eventually realizing our true purpose. The closer we are to discovering our true purpose, the more content we feel about our life because we are putting to use that which we were born to do. We're *living* our true purpose.

Each person is born with the ability to succeed.

Not only is it natural to desire success, success is meant to be *healthy* for you. As you achieve each success, there ought to be improvement in your development as a whole person. You should be benefiting as you strive for success. Here are just a few areas where you should notice improvement over time:

☐ faith

☐ peace of mind

☐ prayer

☐ patience

☐ self-confidence

☐ self-discipline

☐ character

☐ attitude

☐ personality

☐ priorities

☐ lifestyle

☐ quality of friends

☐ quality of environment

For the most part, the world at large tends to equate success with money. In other words, most people think that the more money and possessions they have, the more they are worth and, therefore, the more they should *feel* successful and appear to be successful.

Success is not adding possessions to your life, but subtracting from your monetary desires.

According to most people's standards, the account balance on your bank statement determines your level of success. And the higher the number, the higher the level of success that is assumed. The type of car you drive (whether old, new, domestic, or foreign) or the amount of "bling-bling" you wear (expensive jewelry, diamonds, watches, name-brand clothing and shoes, etc.) determines what socioeconomic status they place you in.

It's a shame that every day, wherever you go— whether it's to the bank, the mall, the restaurant, the grocery store, the school, or the business meeting— most people automatically judge based on appearance alone. They quickly place you in a socioeconomic class: poor, middle, or rich. In most cases, this kind of judging will affect how people treat or mistreat each other.

Although the world has its defining factors of what success is, *you* and *only you* are the final determining factor for what your level of success is or will become based on *your* own standards. Don't let the world define success for you.

How do YOU define success? What does it mean to you?

_____

_____

_____

_____

_____

_____

_____

_____

_____

_____

_____

_____

_____

_____

Is this your own definition of success? Where did your idea of what it means to be successful come from?

_____

_____

_____

_____

_____

_____

_____

_____

_____

_____

Success is a choice; it doesn't happen by chance.

In the beginning of my music career, things weren't always peaches and cream. I didn't just make a record and instantly became a hit, selling over seventy-five million records. Radio stations weren't quick to play my music, magazine editors weren't knocking down my door to interview me, and record stores weren't enthusiastic about selling or promoting my music.

Since I was "different," there were barriers before me that I had to rise above. In the music industry, there were critics who said negative things about me because the style of my music was unlike that of the recording artists that were popular at the time. People said that I was "country" just because I have a southern accent. I wasn't always the headliner for the concerts. Actually, I started out as the opening act, which usually meant "no pay." Southern rap music wasn't trendy at the time. Although I was met with much resistance, I made up my mind to *never give up*.

Picture me on a tour bus in 1995 with a bunch of West Coast artists. My brother and I were the only artists from the South. We were the opening act, and they wouldn't even play our music on the bus. Not only did we have to gain the respect of our peers, we had to establish a fan base larger than just the South. It was easy for my brother and me to perform at the concerts in the South because they were accustomed to the sound of our music. However, when it came to performing as the opening acts in areas outside the South, it was like being thrown into the lion's den.

At one particular concert, I casually told the promoter that I was from the "country," and he didn't want to let me on stage because he thought I might do a country song. Eventually, we were able to assure him that we were not going to sing a country song at a rap concert and instigate a riot. Finally, we hit the stage and started to perform. The crowd of people just stared at us; they didn't respond to the music at all. My brother turned to me and said, "Man, let's just go home." But in the midst of the thousands of people in the stands, I spotted one guy in the crowd. I don't know if this guy was drunk or crazy, but he was dancing like this was the best music he had ever heard. So we played for him, and I said to my brother, "One day, we're going to turn that one guy into millions of fans."

I realized that we were out of our element. Nevertheless, I refused to give up. I understood that it would take some time, more promotions, additional opportunities, and extra faith to create a massive fan base for the future. I learned that you must always seek some sign of positive in a negative situation, and then stay focused on that positive until it multiplies and overpowers the negative.

Success is getting up one more time than you fall.

I stayed true to myself and believed in myself. And I pressed forward. I refused to believe anything the world was trying to feed me that was contrary to my dream. If I had listened to those people—family members, radio stations, hip-hop critics, and everybody else that had something negative to say—where would I be right now? Well, one thing is for sure. You wouldn't be reading my book.

I've discovered through personal experience that as the days, weeks, months, and years go by . . . changes in your life will occur *with* or *without* your efforts; time inevitably changes things. It's up to you to continually define "success" for yourself and then create goals that will keep you on track toward your ultimate purpose.

For example, one of my goals was to establish my own record company, No Limit Records, and sell millions of records. *With my efforts*, I've successfully achieved that goal; my record company has sold over seventy-five million records. As time has passed, *without my efforts*, the ability to download music from the Internet has dramatically changed the music industry. As a result, I've had to set new goals to achieve a higher level of success in a "new" time.

Nothing is forever. I'm a firm believer of, "Once you've reached your goal, it's time to set a new one!" Therefore, your new goal will set the standard for your definition of success. As time changes, your goals, your desires, and your circumstances change. With each change, you—and only you—must modify your definition of success so that you continuously make progress toward your true purpose in life.

Success has nothing to do with luck.
You create your own success.

It's your turn to look into yourself and begin to define exactly what *success* means to *you*, so that you can start, continue, or restart your plan toward success immediately. Don't get lost in life by conforming yourself to other people's opinions. If you don't set *your own* standards for success, someone else most definitely will.

In what specific areas of your life do you have a desire to be successful?

_____

_____

_____

_____

_____

_____

_____

_____

_____

_____

_____

What is your ultimate goal in life? What legacy do you want to leave behind?

_____

_____

_____

_____

_____

_____

_____

_____

_____

_____

_____

What are your short-term goals (up to one year) and your long-term goals (up to five years)? Do your short-term goals relate to your long-term goals? If so, how?

_____

_____

_____

_____

_____

_____

_____

_____

_____

_____

Are the goals you just wrote down really YOUR goals or are they someone else's (i.e., parents, grandparents, spouse, siblings, friends)? If they're someone else's, what are YOUR goals?

_____

_____

_____

_____

_____

_____

_____

Do you believe in yourself? Do you know you have what it takes to reach the highest level of success?

_____

_____

_____

_____

_____

_____

_____

Remember . . .

You are as successful as you make up
your own mind to be.

My thoughts, my ideas, my questions, my answers, my affirmations, and my revelations for *Chapter 2: What is SUCCESS?*

_____

_____

_____

_____

_____

_____

_____

_____

_____

_____

_____

_____

_____

_____

_____

_____

_____

_____

_____

_____

_____

_____

_____

Chapter Three

What is YOUR MOTIVE for SUCCESS?

Why do you want to be successful? *What* is the driving force in your life? *How* do you use your motivation to help you successfully achieve your goals?

*Motives are circumstances
that influence people to react in a certain way.*

My initial motivation for success came from my childhood experiences, living in an environment defeated by poverty, lack of education, domestic violence, homicide, drug abuse, and lawlessness.

I grew up in the ghetto, the notorious "Calliope" projects in New Orleans, the housing development that gave New Orleans its nickname, "Murder Capital of the World." My mother was on welfare with five of us kids. We owned nothing. We were dirt poor. When it was time to eat, we shared our plates because there was not enough food for all of us.

You're never too young to be successful.

My career in entrepreneurship began when I was six years old. I remember collecting aluminum cans from the grocery stores, my parents' workplace, and anywhere else my parents would take me. However, when I was seven years old, I got really creative in discovering ways to create income. On my way to the grocery stores, I noticed that some of the senior citizens from my neighborhood needed help carrying their grocery bags back to their homes. They knew me because we lived in the same neighborhood, so I'd offer my assistance and they would, in turn, bless me with a tip.

Eventually, I started going to the grocery store for them and delivering their groceries to their doorstep. Soon after that, I learned how to cut grass. I would earn anywhere from two to five dollars, sometimes even ten dollars just for cutting my neighbors' grass! Opportunities for success are *always* available.

At this point in your life, what motivates you to be successful?

_____

_____

_____

_____

_____

_____

_____

_____

_____

_____

_____

_____

_____

_____

_____

At age nine, I made up my mind that I was not going to settle for a life of poverty—either for myself or for my family. And since I was the oldest of my siblings, I believed in my heart that I had to be the one to make that change for my family. I had to get out there and do something. But at such a young age, what could I do that would make any difference? Well, I remember my grandmother used to say to me:

"The poorest person in the world is a person without a dream."

So my first dream was for my family to have a better life. I was determined that no matter what I became involved in, I would refuse to settle for mediocrity. I made a commitment to be the best I could be, at anything and everything that I needed to do! I believed that was the only way I could contribute to help my parents and make a difference for my family.

Ordinary person (at any age) + Extra effort = Extraordinary success

I was determined to be an honor student and get the best grades in my class. And in case I was going to be a professional athlete, I was determined to be the captain of my football team and basketball team. Although I was surrounded by peers who were using drugs, I remained sober. I knew that I couldn't get a decent job or play sports if I couldn't pass the drug tests.

I was just an ordinary kid putting forth extra effort. With focused determination, I achieved all of the goals I set during my childhood and adolescent years.

Do you have a dream? What is it? What are you doing today to make your dream come true?

_____

_____

_____

_____

_____

_____

_____

_____

_____

_____

_____

_____

_____

_____

I truly believe that if I had not been poverty stricken, I would not have had the passion to make a difference for my family. My passion derived from my hunger—literally! It's easier for someone who's living comfortably with minimal worries to just lie down and sleep all day. Someone who's starving has no choice but to get up, get out there, and do something!

You can tell when someone has passion;
you don't have to wake them up in the morning.
They're already awake and ready to go.

When I was eleven years old, I broke my hip playing football at school. The doctor said that I would never be able to walk again. I clearly remember looking down at that big white cast on my little body and thinking to myself, *I am **not** going to stay like this!* As a matter of fact, the first time I got up out of that hospital bed, I did it on my own. My parents had to work because we couldn't afford for them to take any time off. This motivated me to get up and exercise on my own. I could have easily just lain down, given up, and said it was over. That's passion—to just get up! To not lie down, to not give up!

Are you passionate about reaching your goal? How passionate?

_____
_____
_____
_____
_____
_____
_____
_____

_____

_____

_____

_____

_____

_____

_____

Do your thoughts and actions support your goals? If your answer is "yes," how so? If "no," why not?

_____

_____

_____

_____

_____

_____

_____

_____

_____

_____

_____

_____

_____

Motive ignites passion,
and passion gives birth to success.

I remember not being able to go to the prom in high school because I didn't have any transportation. I couldn't borrow someone's car because none of my family members or friends had one. As a teenager, it was such a disappointment not to be able to go to the prom, go school shopping, wear new shoes, have nice clothes, or go to the store and buy food when I was hungry like some of the other kids could. Not having these things, no matter how small or insignificant it may seem to some people, was a huge motivating factor for me to make the necessary changes so that I could afford those things.

In my early twenties, I came into some money from my grandmother's lawsuit for my grandfather's "unlawful death." I took that money and made my first financial investment: I bought a record store that was going out of business in an urban community. I fixed it up and promoted it throughout the city. As a result, my record store was a booming success and, for the first time, I began to experience a comfortable lifestyle.

I thought I was doing pretty well until a tragedy struck: My brother was killed. It became a powerful motivator that drove me out of my comfort zone. I had my family to look out for, and I knew that I couldn't remain stagnant any longer.

I refused to stand by and witness my loved ones perish; I couldn't allow it. So I implemented a plan for my life that included major changes. I realized I had to take my already successful business to an even higher level of financial success in order to put my family and myself in a better position.

This was actually the first of many experiences that motivated me to never settle in my successes. Life is unpredictable. No matter who you are, no one is immune to life's problems. You have to prepare for unforeseen events because they can knock you down pretty hard if you're not ready for them. You can't control everything that happens to you, but you do have control over how you prepare for the unknown and how you react to it when it happens.

Never settle
in your successes.

My grandfather always said, "A true soldier is prepared for war in a time of peace." This inspires me every single day to be smart about preparing for my next level of success. There is an appointed time for everything in life. I have only begun to lay the foundation needed to prepare for my future.

Although my brother getting killed caused me a lot of pain, I am grateful that God enables me to use the tragedies in my life to make changes for the better. I have learned to take responsibility for my own actions, not to blame others.

My father also told me:

"If it doesn't kill you, it will only make you stronger."

So I chose to stop and look at those obstacles in my life and say to myself, "What can I do to make things better and not worse?" I didn't waste much time complaining or worrying. I honestly believe that God has already equipped us with the talents and abilities to be successful in this life. We only need to take our focus off the oppositions and center our attention on solutions and opportunities. There's also a biblical saying that I know: "What they mean for evil, God is able to use for good."

Some people need a driving force for motivation. They need a motive because if there is no "earth-shattering" occurrence in their life, then there is no burning desire to make things right.

A tragedy or hardship can inspire motive if you allow it, but not everyone is inspired by the desire to overcome obstacles. There are some people who are inspired by positive influences, an awareness of possibility. This often comes in the form of a role model the person admires.

Back when I was in high school, Oprah Winfrey

was the most successful black person I could identify myself with because she was always right there in front of me on television. So I would always say to myself, "If Oprah Winfrey could do it, I can do it. She's black and she's a woman; God knows what she's been through to attain her level of success. She's living proof that it's possible."

In addition to Oprah, my list of role models includes Arnold Schwarzenegger, Bill Gates, Donald Trump, Martin Luther King, Mohammed Ali, Willie Nelson, and of course Jesus. Each one has deeply inspired me, giving me the motivational encouragement to reach my maximum potential and continue to fulfill my own unique purpose in life.

Role models make it possible for us to believe in ourselves and to know that success is indeed attainable. We all need a role model to enthuse us in one way or another.

Who are your role models? How do they inspire you?

_____

_____

_____

_____

_____

_____

*Every successful person has a motive
that fuels his or her passion for success.*

Motive *instigates* passion; passion *initiates* success. Passion will propel you to make changes that you may have otherwise never thought to make. Every time my motive changes, my expectation of success elevates. As a result, my desire for a higher level of success intensifies.

The passion that drives me now is something bigger than me, my family, and the other people around me. It's about living with purpose and creating success that benefits others, even long after I leave this earth.

*You have discovered your purpose
when the vision of your dream
is constant in your mind and heart.*

I discovered my life's true purpose after Hurricane Katrina. I knew that no matter what I was going through in my own life, I had to figure out how to be there for other people—my family, my friends, and the many others who lost everything due to the hurricane. So many people that I knew were affected by this tragedy in one way or another. People lost loved ones, their homes, their businesses, and their hope. I quickly found myself in a leadership position because I realized my help was desperately needed.

Before the hurricane, I was dealing only with my own issues: tax problems, bogus lawsuits, and cunning business associates. It was using up a lot of my time and wasting a lot of money. There was no way I could handle all that chaos on my own. My back was against the wall because I had already sought the help of experts in every field, yet nothing was improving. I realized the help I needed could not come from people alone; I needed God's help. This is the time in my life where my relationship with God became stronger. I started reading the Bible because I was looking for answers. Through studying the Bible, I learned how to praise and pray. I praised Him for all that He has already done in my life, and I prayed for Him to guide me in the right direction and to give me wisdom and strength. I learned how to become more spiritual and more appreciative.

I discovered that if I truly desired to be successful, I had to play my role—use the abilities that God gave me and share them with others. If I was willing to use my talents and be there for others, God would always be there for me. He would guide me to be in the right place at the right time, to meet the right people, to make the right decisions.

It took making millions of dollars, losing it, making some of it back, and then seeing the devastation of Hurricane Katrina for me to recognize my life's true purpose: to use my God-given talents and abilities for the benefit of all. One of my goals that relates to my ultimate purpose is to help rebuild our communities. I want to help kids and their families build a foundation that will last so they don't die young in the ghetto, kill each other, do drugs, or go hungry. I want to help provide opportunities for them to grow, to get an education and mature out of that street mentality.

Does your goal benefit others besides yourself? If so, explain how.

_____

_____

_____

_____

_____

_____

_____

_____

_____

_____

_____

_____

_____

_____

_____

_____

I didn't make it out of poverty in vain. I am obligated to share the wisdom I gained from my experiences so that others will have the advantage that I didn't. My vision is that every community has access to financial education and opportunities that provide economic stability and success.

At times, we may not have control over our circumstances, but we do have the authority to use them as a motivating force to do good.

Begin to guarantee your success by starting right where you are at this moment. Don't imprison yourself by focusing on past failures or past successes. *Use those experiences.* Learn from them and let them prepare and motivate you for your next level of success. Keep looking forward and envisioning your goal. Every single day, see yourself reaching your goal. Press on until you achieve it, and then set a new one.

Your motive should inspire you to be passionate about your desire for success. If you're not passionate, it's time to reevaluate your motives—the reasons for your goal.

My thoughts, my ideas, my questions, my answers, my affirmations, and my revelations for *Chapter 3: What is YOUR MOTIVE for SUCCESS?*

_____

_____

_____

_____

_____

_____

_____

_____

_____

_____

_____

_____

_____

_____

_____

_____

_____

_____

_____

_____

_____

CHAPTER FOUR

DOES YOUR ATTITUDE ATTRACT SUCCESS?

What is attitude? Why is *attitude* vital to success? Most people have no idea just how powerfully their attitude affects the direction of their lives. A **motive** has the ability to *inspire* passion for success just as an **attitude** has the ability to *attract* success.

Your attitude is powerful;
it can make you or break you.

Attitude is expressed in several ways: how you *think, feel,* or *act.* The attitude of how you *think* is the most powerful because it directly influences how you feel and how you act. Positive thinking produces positive feelings and positive actions. Therefore, the attitude that you project most of the time will determine the kind of life you will have.

Your thoughts (*the attitude of the way you think*) are revealed to others through your actions. It works like karma; what goes around comes around. For example, if you project a positive attitude most of the time, then most of the time positive things consequentially happen to you. Unfortunately, it works exactly the same way with a negative attitude. A negative attitude reaps negative results.

The great news is that you have the power to create the destiny you desire by controlling the attitude you carry. You can make life *easier* for yourself Why not have an attitude that attracts success?

Here are the **7 ATTITUDES of SUCCESS:**

1. **Self-Confidence** → Believing in yourself and your abilities

2. **Self-Discipline** → Doing what is necessary to achieve a goal

3. **Self-Motivation** → Inspiring yourself without the need to be prompted by others

4. **Respect** → Treating others as you desire to be treated

5. **Team Player** → Cooperating with others to achieve a common goal

6. **Understanding** → Increasing knowledge by educating yourself in the areas you wish to succeed

7. **Integrity** → Doing what is right—morally, ethically, and legally

Take a moment now to look closely at your attitudes, to see if they're attracting success to you or keeping you from it.

Do you believe in yourself? Which of your abilities are you most confident in? When do you feel most confident?

_____

_____

_____

_____

_____

_____

_____

_____

_____

Are you doing something *each day* that requires self-discipline and is moving you toward your goal?

_____

_____

_____

_____

_____

_____

_____

_____

_____

_____

_____

_____

Are you passionate enough about your goal to motivate yourself?

_____

_____

_____

_____

_____

_____

_____

How do you want to be treated? Does it match how you treat other people?

_____
_____
_____
_____
_____
_____
_____
_____

How are cooperation and teamwork necessary in order for you to achieve your goal?

_____
_____
_____
_____
_____
_____
_____
_____

What do you need to understand better? Are you educating yourself?

_____
_____
_____

_____

_____

_____

_____

_____

How is your integrity (or someone else's) making a difference in your life right now?

_____

_____

_____

_____

_____

_____

_____

_____

_____

Does your attitude attract success? These attitudes are learned, and you have control over your destiny because you have complete authority over the way you think. If the way you think (*your present attitude*) is not attracting success, you have the ability to change your thinking. You can't change it overnight, but you can make a difference each day as you train yourself to think positive thoughts that attract success.

Controlling your attitude is vitally important.

When you are able to control your attitude (*the way that you think*), you gain complete control over your feelings and your actions. This type of self-discipline leads to success. Most people have what I call a *situational attitude*, an attitude that fluctuates depending on the situation. Someone who has a *situational attitude* does not control their feelings or actions. This person is more likely to react to a negative situation in a negative way, which results in the situation only getting worse. Success is impossible to achieve with this type of attitude. Never allow a situation to dictate your attitude!

A positive attitude
will prevail over any negative situation.

As you and I both know, life is unpredictable. You never know what circumstances life may bring. Have you ever heard of the saying, "Sometimes beautiful gifts come in ugly packages"? Well, that's life! Opposition knocks on everyone's door from time to time. But a person who has control over their attitude has the ability to turn that opposition into an opportunity.

Allow oppositions to strengthen you
rather than weaken you.

My ability to control all of my 7 Attitudes of Success was tested when I appeared on the national television show, *Dancing with the Stars*. My son, Romeo, had a contractual agreement to perform on the show, but he was unable to fulfill his obligations due to an unforeseen injury.

I wanted to show my son the importance of *integrity*. When you make a commitment, it's imperative that you carry it out. Since it was impossible for him to dance with his injury, I agreed to perform in his place. I had never ballroom danced a day in my life, and I come from a whole different hip-hop generation that gives me a totally different fan base. I had to quickly figure out how I could make this work for us without jeopardizing my already established reputation with the hip-hop community.

Since I knew appearing on the show might lead the whole world to see me in a different light, my first thought was that whatever I did, I had to be myself! Being *self-confident* (secure and comfortable with yourself) can help you achieve your goals and rise above any barriers that you may encounter.

The network and I gave each other mutual *respect*. I came out of my world and entered into theirs, so I had to play their game by their rules. Nevertheless, we were able to compromise along the way. Since I was not going to wear the typical wardrobe they expected the male dancers to wear, I had to *motivate myself* to create an urban style with a crossover look. Inspired by the movie *Scarface*, I put together all the suits that the character Tony Montana wore. Then another conflict arose; I refused to wear those painful ballroom shoes. So I thought to myself, *Why not wear my own P. Miller shoes?* It gave me a hip-hop flavor while doing the ballroom dancing, which allowed me to conquer the best of both worlds (not to mention, advertise my P. Miller brand) . . . another example of turning an opposition into an opportunity.

I'm a strong believer in never allowing a person or business venture to take you out of your character. I had to look at myself in the mirror and say, *I don't mind playing by their rules, as long as I can be myself.*

In order to prepare for the show, I had to be a **team player** with a lot of **self-discipline**. Ballroom dancing was simply something that I would never do just to be doing it. I was out of my element. I have to take my hat off to my trainer because she was extra patient with me. Keep in mind, the media was already questioning my dancing abilities. My trainer and I were both determined to be successful, so we were dedicated to teamwork. We practiced, I allowed myself to discover something new, and I learned to appreciate it. **Knowledge** and **understanding** are definite keys to success. I gave my trainer and the network a lot of respect. In turn, my experience with them was remarkably unforgettable.

While I was the underdog on that show, the audience showed me so much love. The other dance competitors even complained that it was a popularity contest instead of a dance contest. But the audience continued to vote for me, keeping me on the show for a shocking four weeks! By the way, I just want to say thank you again to all of you who voted for me!

During the portion of the show where the judges critique your dance performance before giving you a score, one of the judges made an outlandish, inappropriate remark to me on national television. I maintained my composure, acknowledged his comment with a slight nod and grin, but I gave his personal opinion no merit. I didn't become angry, nor did I let his negativity sabotage my positive attitude. When you take your eyes off the prize, you end up where you don't want to be. I could have let the judge's comment get to me, or I could have responded with equal negativity. I chose to make light of it instead. By keeping a positive attitude, I was able to obtain endorsements and increase my fan base.

You don't have to be a victim of your circumstances unless you choose to be. It doesn't matter where you came from; what matters is where you are headed. I am well aware that I have the ability to control my attitude—and so do you! It may take some practice. Believe me, I've had to practice controlling my attitude for years. If I had faced that same situation just a few years ago, being harshly criticized on national television, the outcome would have been disastrous.

> *Nobody can make you feel inferior*
> *without your permission.*

I know that it's a challenge to keep a positive attitude when it seems like the odds are against you. People may make attempts to destroy your *self-confidence*, distract you from *self-motivation*, test your *self-discipline*, deter you from being a *team player*, diminish your *integrity*, *misunderstand* you, and/or *disrespect* you. But stand firm and keep your attitude positive.

> *A challenge is only the warning signal*
> *that success is near.*

Looking back at my life and at my present circumstances, I've come to realize how powerful the impact of a person's attitude truly is. Your attitude is much more important than your appearance, your skills, and your education. No matter how bad your past experiences or your present circumstances may be, you should not give any power to it over your present attitude.

I know now that you can tell if a person is living for

a purpose or not, just by observing their attitude. And I've come to understand that your attitude toward life will determine life's attitude toward you.

It is our own individual responsibility to take authority over our attitude. Life is too short to waste time and energy trying to change the past or the people around you. You only have the power and authority to change and control yourself and your own attitude.

I highly recommend that any person who desires to live *successfully* and *on purpose* selectively gathers a personalized collection of words of wisdom, biblical scriptures, and positive affirmations that support their mission—their ultimate plan, goal, and purpose.

On a personal note, here is one of many of my favorite scriptures that I meditate on, especially when my attitude is being tried.

"So do not throw away your confidence;
it will be richly rewarded."
—Hebrews 10:35

My thoughts, my ideas, my questions, my answers, my affirmations, and my revelations for *Chapter 4: Does Your ATTITUDE Attract SUCCESS?*

_____

_____

_____

_____

_____

_____

_____

_____

_____

_____

_____

_____

_____

_____

_____

_____

_____

_____

_____

_____

_____

_____

_____

_____

Chapter Five

What is HINDERING your SUCCESS?

What is a hindrance? How do you overcome hindrances?

A hindrance to success is anything or anyone that prevents or makes it difficult for you to achieve success. These hindrances are obstacles, whether physical or mental (*a negative attitude*), that interfere with your ability to achieve success by holding you back, slowing you down, or blocking you completely. A hindrance is simply a *distraction* designed to place limitations on your ability to succeed. It's a *diversion* intended to keep you from accomplishing your ultimate plan, goal, and purpose.

As I mentioned earlier, knowledge is key. You can overcome hindrances once you understand how hindrances operate. There are various forms of hindrances to success, and they often come in clever disguises. The good news is that you can victoriously conquer each hindrance when you're able to identify it without delay.

With the right attitude, hindrances to your success only make your achievements that much greater. Any time you make an attempt to bring about success in anything worthwhile, you can almost always expect hindrances to come before you.

Knowledge will help you see the opportunities in your oppositions.

Let's look at the different hindrances to success so that you can immediately recognize and conquer them. In general, the main cause of a hindrance is the *lack* of something. There are *seven bindrances to success*, and there are *seven elements of lack* out of which the hindrances are birthed.

7 Elements of Lack	7 Hindrances to Success
1. Lack of Self-Confidence	1. Fear
2. Lack of Self-Discipline	2. Procrastination
3. Lack of Knowledge	3. Past Failures and Successes
4. Lack of Education	4. Wasting Time
5. Lack of Self-Motivation	5. Comfort
6. Lack of Direction	6. Negative Attitude
7. Lack of Guidance	7. Negative Environment

As we take a closer look at each of the hindrances, you will see their negative effects. You will also notice that these hindrances negatively cause and affect other hindrances. At the same time, every hindrance presents an opportunity to improve your condition.

1. Fear

In my opinion, fear is the number one hindrance to success. Fear is the result of ignorance. And ignorance is caused by a *lack of knowledge and/or education*.

Fear causes you to worry about the unknown of what lies ahead: *Will it be a success or will it fail?* It can torment you, causing you to be worried about things that are really a waste of time and energy: *What if this happens, that happens, or nothing happens?* Fear is also known as "**F**alse **E**vidence **A**ppearing **R**eal." It's only an idea or thought that you are afraid of. Fear is an anticipation of a negative outcome, an expectation of negative results.

Indecisiveness develops into a hindrance because it is caused by *fear*. A prolonged habit of indecisiveness is dangerous because you become reluctant to make decisions. The inability to make decisions—refusing to take any action and rejecting any opportunity toward productiveness—will drain your enthusiasm and willingness to succeed. Sometimes you can be your own worst enemy because you confuse, contradict, and question yourself repeatedly. There are three kinds of people: (1) people that *watch* things happen, (2) people that *wonder* what will happen, and (3) people that *make* things happen. So, which kind will you choose to be?

An indecisive person won't *make things happen* because they suffer from a severe case of *self-doubt*. Unfortunately, they fail to succeed because they do not know exactly what they want to succeed in. In many cases, they *waste time* trying to do everything but the *right* thing, or they start things but don't finish them. They allow *fear* to take hold of them and worry themselves to the point of inaction.

What are you afraid of? Is fear ("False Evidence Appearing Real") hindering your ability to succeed? What step will you take to overcome your fears?

_____

_____

_____

_____

_____

_____

_____

_____

_____

_____

_____

_____

_____

_____

_____

_____

Pursue success in spite of fear . . .
and guaranteed victory will be near!

2. Procrastination

Success is often postponed due to procrastination. Your dream only lingers. Days turn into weeks, weeks turn into months, and months turn into years. Procrastination will attack all areas of your life. It can exist in your finances, your marriage, goals for your children, and the development of your full potential. Procrastination can eventually ruin your credit, your health, your relationships, your business . . . the list goes on.

If you just do it,
you don't have to worry about getting it done.

Procrastination can also cause you to miss out. You may see your idea or invention come to pass right before your very eyes in someone else's life. It causes delays in your life that cause delays in your ability to take care of business.

Procrastination is a deadly habit that only becomes worse. It's "deadly" because it can kill every opportunity that leads to any type of success.

Excuses are a product of *procrastination*. These excuses are given to explain the reason for a person's failure to succeed. An excuse is habitually used to justify the basis for why the *pursuit of success* is a *mission impossible.* So they give up and avoid even trying. You'll notice, people can get really creative when it comes to making excuses.

They focus their time and energy on the reasons for their *inability to succeed* when they should focus their time and energy on their *actual ability to accomplish something* by making a plan and working at it. They conjure up long lists of excuses why they cannot make something happen or why it's impossible for them to succeed. They convince themselves and therefore completely handicap themselves.

Do you make excuses for why you "can't" succeed or reach your goal? If so, what are they? Are you ready to stop making excuses, to stop procrastinating, and take just one step toward your goal? What would that step be?

_____

_____

_____

_____

_____

_____

_____

_____

_____

_____

_____

_____

_____

Procrastination is a definite sign of fear.

Review your goals and establish your priorities. Build up your motivation and commitment. The first step is to change your way of thinking. Then work to create small successes and build on them.

3. **Past Failures and Successes**

Dwelling on the past causes you to live for the past, distracting you from being fully productive in the present and sidetracking you from preparing for the future. Past experiences, whether successes or failures, should be left right where they are—*in the past.*

*Past failures are only stepping stones
for future successes.*

Fearing an undesirable outcome (*past failures*) and making an attempt to relive, revive, or repeat the past (*past successes*) is definitely a ***waste of time*** and energy. This becomes a hindrance because it will hamper your potential to grow.

Failure is success
when you learn from it.

On the other hand, it is necessary to confront your past failures and successes. Analyze them so that you can learn from the experiences. By examining your past failures, you can prevent repetition of past mistakes. And by studying your past successes, you can enhance your vision for a plan toward your future successes. This is a sure way to exercise your own power to turn something negative into a positive!

Do you focus on your past, or on your future? How can your past failures and successes help you reach your future goals?

_____

_____

_____

_____

_____

_____

_____

_____

_____

_____

_____

_____

_____

_____

_____

_____

_____

_____

_____

_____

_____

_____

_____

_____

_____

_____

*Your purpose in life is much more significant
than your past failures and successes.*

4. Wasting Time

Money can be multiplied, but time cannot. Once you spend time, it's gone, and there is no getting it back. Everyone has the opportunity to spend time, and when they do, they either invest it or waste it. Sometimes they lose control of how they spend their time and allow people or things that don't contribute to their goal to use up their time.

Distractions cause you to *waste time*. A distraction is anything or anyone in your life that keeps you from being productive and achieving your goal. Some of us have a knack for distracting ourselves. These distractions come in many forms. Sometimes you can be distracted even by doing something "good." More important than doing what is "good," you must do what is "right." We occupy ourselves with things that don't relate to our ultimate plan, goal, and purpose. Keep in mind, a distraction is *anything* and *everything* that prevents you from doing what is most beneficial to you and your achievement of your goals.

A lack of time management skills can cause you to waste precious time. Our time on this earth is unpredictable, temporary, and very limited. Don't waste your time trying to be like other people or just following along with what others are doing. Learn to manage your precious time wisely, avoiding distractions and staying focused on your goals.

How do you use your time? Do you let yourself get easily distracted or do you stay focused on your goals? Does how you spend your time show that you understand your time is valuable?

_____

_____

_____

_____

_____

_____

_____

_____

_____

_____

_____

_____

_____

_____

_____

_____

_____

_____

_____

_____

_____

*Distractions are anything and everything
that keep you from your goal.*

5. **Comfort**

Comfort is the most deceiving hindrance of all. It hinders your future successes because it keeps you stagnant in your present circumstances. This is actually another form of *wasting time*. You fool yourself into believing that you have already fulfilled your purpose in life.

Your false sense of contentment disables you; it prevents you from discovering your maximum potential and *distracts* you from reaching your highest level of success. Settling within the comfort zone of your present state of success will impair your creativity and rob you of your motivation for any future goals.

A successful life never ends in a state of comfortable living. If you do not reach your maximum potential and live a purposeful life, then you have aborted your life's mission. This is a sad scenario because your unique purpose has died with you.

Do you let yourself slip into a comfort zone and stay there, or do you continually push forward toward greater success? Give an example.

Your true purpose is designed to outlive you. In the end, when you have fulfilled your true purpose, your accomplishments will continue to be alive in this world, still benefiting others.

Don't be satisfied with a mediocre life.

6. Negative Attitude

It takes patience and persistence to defeat this hindrance. A negative attitude is the "kryptonite" to your success—it will weaken any opportunity that leads you toward success. This is where you become your greatest enemy. Giving yourself permission to shelter a negative attitude is simply suicidal.

Self-doubt is a consequence of a negative attitude. This is a hindrance that you alone place upon yourself. It's a form of self-destruction. This will also cause you to be *indecisive, waste time*, and live in *fear*. Your negative thoughts will produce your negative feelings, negative actions, and ultimately result in disappointment, frustration, regret, and the inevitable *failure to succeed.*

Do you let self-doubt get in the way of success? If so, what step can you take to change that?

_____

_____

_____

_____

_____

_____

_____

_____

_____

_____

_____

_____

_____

The *unwillingness to forgive* is a byproduct of a negative attitude. Most people overlook this powerful hindrance; it's often disregarded because of its quiet existence. People underestimate its ability to influence a chain of negative effects. The failure to forgive causes a heavy burden in you. It affects your willingness to trust, preventing you from developing new relationships. It creates a negative vibe that festers and grows within you, preventing positive opportunities from coming into your life.

Are you willing to forgive? If not, how might it be hindering your ability to succeed?

_____

_____

_____

_____

_____

_____

_____

_____

_____

_____

_____

_____

_____

I am not suggesting that you should forget the hurt, pain, or negative experience; I am simply saying to forgive the offender, for your own sake. When you forgive, you destroy the negative barrier inside of you, allowing and attracting constructive opportunities to flow freely and surround you. Therefore, you move on and press forward to success.

The three "Cs"—*Complain, Compare,* and *Covet*— are destructive side effects of a negative attitude.

Complaining, comparing, and coveting are signals of an inevitable negative outcome. These acts are not only a form of *wasting time*, they prevent success. Time and energy are wasted on these acts, therefore hindering your maximum potential.

Do you spend your time complaining, comparing, or coveting? If so, is it bringing about the results you desire?

_____

_____

_____

_____

_____

_____

_____

_____

_____

_____

_____

_____

_____

_____

The *disillusionment of success* is a tricky hindrance caused by ignorance and a lack of guidance and direction. A person who has the *disillusionment of success* has a misconception of what success truly is. They develop this negative attitude (*negative way of thinking*) from misinformation, what they see and hear from other people. As a result, they end up impersonating a "successful" person because they have this picture in their mind of what "success" should look like. They make extreme attempts to only *appear* successful (*e.g., driving an expensive car, wearing expensive jewelry, etc.*) oftentimes living outside of their means. They create a façade, a false identity. Often, they do it for so long, they eventually even fool themselves. They often spend time around other people who also suffer from the ***disillusionment of success***. This only validates their façade and prevents their growth.

> *Establish your own*
> *true definition for success.*

Have you ever experienced the *disillusionment of success*? What does true success mean to you?

_____

_____

_____

_____

_____

_____

_____

_____

_____

_____

The problem with this type of thinking is that it is not reality. It's dangerous because you never reach your maximum potential. You believe you are already successful, when in the true sense of success, you are not. You decide to "fake it 'til you make it." In reality, it doesn't work that way. That's why people often fall off the ladder of success so quickly. The *disillusionment of success* always leads to frustration and disappointment.

> *A seed of negative attitude*
> *will harvest a negative aptitude.*

7. Negative Environment

A negative environment consists of surroundings and situations, including places and people, that nurture or encourage negativity. It could be the neighborhood you live in, your workplace, or a personal or business relationship where negativity lingers. A negative environment puts a *chokehold* on the *breath of life*, limiting your potential for success.

"Dream Killers" are key players in a negative environment. They are everywhere! They could be in your family, at your job, at your in-laws', in your neighborhood, at school, at social clubs, and even at church! What is a "Dream Killer"? It's the imposter that poses as your family member, friend, associate—the one you share your ideas with. In your presence or behind your back, they laugh at you and your goal, whether it involves a business venture, a professional career, or an invention. These pretenders are betting on your failure, wishing for your failure, and not believing that you have what it takes to be a success. They either secretly or openly anticipate your failure.

> ### Don't share your dream with everyone right away.

"Crabs in a Bucket" are the closely related family members and/or friends who have a negative attitude. If they do any of the three "Cs" (*Complain, Compare, or Covet*), it's safe to say that they are co-creators of your negative environment. They're the main reason you're lacking a supportive team. They have made a conscious or subconscious commitment to hold you back, slow you down, or completely block you from success.

When it comes to *"Dream Killers"* and *"Crabs in a Bucket,"* silence is your best protection. If you are unsure whether or not a person has your best interest at heart, hold off on sharing your dream or idea with them. If you choose to share, use discretion; make sure it will be someone who is praying for your success.

Choose your associates wisely.
Make sure they are headed in the same direction;
they must have goals too.

Do you surround yourself with people who push you toward your goals or do you listen to "Dream Killers" and "Crabs in a Bucket"?

_____

_____

_____

_____

_____

_____

Since you tend to become like those you spend time with, spend more time with productive and ambitious people and spend less time with irresponsible or lazy people who are allergic to success. If a person happily and willingly provides all of the reasons why you can't do something or why your goal is impossible to achieve, consider reevaluating your relationship with that person.

Remove yourself as soon as possible from any negative environment. It's impossible to attract success or develop your maximum potential in a condition especially designed for your failure.

You can only be a failure if you fail to try!

As you continue to think about these principles, you will soon discover the origin of any hindrance in your life and can begin to make specific plans to overcome it. Since the cause of every **hindrance** is *lack*, you do not have to be a victim of your circumstances any longer. Once you become aware of your hindrances, you are armed with the knowledge to do something about them.

Make sure you truthfully answered the questions in this chapter so you can turn your obstacles into opportunities. Commit to changing any "lack of" to "an abundance of" and you will no longer be hindering your success. You'll be moving toward it. If you're lacking self-confidence, build it up until you have more than enough of it. If you're lacking self-discipline, practice it *each day* until you've mastered it. If you're lacking knowledge or education, take the time to find resources, experiences, and teachers that will provide you with all the understanding you need. If you're lacking motivation, dig deep until you discover your passion. If you're lacking direction or guidance, surround yourself with people who want to see you succeed and who *know* you have it in you. **You can turn any "lack" into "abundance," therefore turning your obstacles into opportunities.**

My thoughts, my ideas, my questions, my answers, my affirmations, and my revelations for *Chapter 5. What is HINDERING Your SUCCESS?*

_____

_____

_____

_____

_____

_____

_____

_____

_____

_____

_____

_____

_____

_____

_____

_____

_____

_____

_____

_____

_____

_____

CHAPTER SIX

WHAT IS THE **BLUEPRINT** FOR YOUR **SUCCESS?**

The *blueprint for your success* is your plan of action. Do you have a blueprint for your success? If so, is it working for you? Where did you get it from or how did you come up with it? Is it your own blueprint or is it someone else's?

The blueprint for your own success must be exclusive, one of a kind, custom-made by you. No one else can make up a blueprint for *your* success. Sure, you can follow general guidelines and live by universal principles that attract success. But eventually, you must create a unique plan that suits you—your circumstances, your personality, your character, your talents, and your abilities. For that reason, the *quality* of the blueprint for your success depends primarily on your *self-worth*.

*Your ability to achieve success
relies predominantly on your self-worth.*

In order for you to take action toward success, your self-worth must be intact so that your blueprint can be used effectively during the building process of your successes. Therefore, it is imperative that the quality of your blueprint is as high as possible so that you avoid wasting your time, your money, your energy, and your life.

Do you know what you are worth? Is it of **high** value or **low** value? Are you placing a dollar amount on your worth? What is the basis of your self-worth? How does your self-worth relate to your success?

Your self-worth is the perception you have of yourself based on your confidence in the significant value of yourself as a whole person. *Take a moment to reflect on what you just read.*

It is vitally important that you completely understand the full concept of your self-worth because it directly influences the personal blueprint for your success. In other words, it directly affects your individual potential for success.

There are seven influential factors that contribute to the development of your self-worth. Take a look at these dynamic factors that form the structure of your self-worth.

7 Factors that Influence SELF-WORTH

1. Self-Assessment

2. Self-Image

3. Self-Concept

4. Self-Respect

5. Self-Esteem

6. Self-Actualization

7. Self-Empowerment

As mentioned in the first chapter of this book, the first step is always awareness. So let's start by finding out what you believe you are worth at this time. As we explore the seven factors that influence self-worth, write down what *immediately* comes to mind after you read the explanation for each factor. Just write down your thoughts as they come—words and phrases that describe how you see yourself and how you *feel* about yourself. Don't use your words to hide your thoughts because, in reality, your actions will reveal them. **Rather than wasting your time censoring yourself,** just be honest with yourself! Give yourself at *least* five minutes to just keep writing.

1. **Self-Assessment** →A process of self-evaluation; a reviewing of the habits of the mind, body, and spirit

_____

_____

_____

_____

_____

_____

_____

_____

_____

_____

_____

_____

These exercises will greatly benefit you only if you actually do them. If you truly desire to get the most out of reading this book, make sure now that you have done the previous exercise before you continue to read on. Remember to be completely honest with yourself and just write *whatever* comes to mind.

Your thoughts are influential,
but your words have creative power.

2. **Self-Image** → A self-portrait that you have painted for yourself; the picture or idea that you have of yourself; how you see yourself in your own mind

_____

_____

_____

_____

_____

_____

_____

_____

_____

_____

_____

3. **Self-Concept** → The inner picture that you have of yourself as a whole, including your capabilities, intelligence, significance, and attractiveness

_____

_____

_____

_____

_____

_____

_____

_____

_____

4. **Self-Respect** → Belief in your integrity, your dignity, and your worthiness

_____

_____

_____

_____

_____

_____

_____

_____

_____

_____

5. **Self-Esteem** → Confidence in yourself, acknowledgment of your own significant value that demands respect and merit because it is well deserved

_____

_____

_____

_____

_____

_____

_____

_____

_____

_____

6. **Self-Actualization** → The successful development of talents, skills, and abilities

_____

_____

_____

_____

_____

_____

_____

_____

_____

_____

_____

_____

_____

_____

7. **Self-Empowerment** → Activating your untapped power within; taking authority over yourself; inspiring and motivating yourself to reach your maximum potential and fulfill your true purpose

_____

_____

_____

_____

_____

_____

_____

_____

_____

_____

Your level of success is directly influenced by the value that you place on your self-worth. Notice I said that you are the one who places a value on your own self-worth. The higher in value your self-worth is, the more success you will achieve.

Your unique blueprint
is a reflection of your self-worth.

Do you see yourself as "successful"? Explain.

_____

_____

_____

_____

_____

_____

_____

_____

_____

_____

_____

_____

_____

_____

_____

_____

_____

_____

_____

_____

Do you see yourself becoming more successful? Explain.

_____

_____

_____

_____
_____
_____
_____
_____
_____
_____
_____
_____
_____
_____
_____
_____
_____
_____
_____
_____
_____
_____
_____
_____
_____

Sooner or later,
you become what you constantly envision.

Do you believe you have what it takes (capability, intelligence, significance, etc.) to reach the highest level of success? Why or why not?

_____

_____

_____

_____

_____

_____

_____

_____

_____

"As a man thinks in his heart . . . so is he."
—Proverbs 3:27

Do you respect yourself? Do the people you know respect you? Give reasons for your answer.

_____

_____

_____

_____

_____

_____

_____

99

Does your daily behavior show self-respect, integrity, dignity, and self-worth? Explain.

_____

_____

_____

_____

_____

_____

_____

_____

_____

_____

_____

Do the people you associate with on a daily basis have self-respect, integrity, dignity, and self-worth? If not, why do you associate with them?

_____

_____

_____

_____

_____

_____

_____

_____

_____

_____

_____

_____

_____

_____

_____

Do you think success is attainable without respect, integrity, dignity, and self-worth? Explain.

_____

_____

_____

_____

_____

_____

_____

_____

_____

_____

_____

_____

_____

_____

Are your daily thoughts and actions expressed with confidence? If yes, how so?

_____

_____

_____

_____

_____

_____

_____

_____

_____

_____

_____

Do you believe that you are significant and important? Why or why not?

_____

_____

_____

_____

_____

_____

_____

_____

_____

_____

Do you truly believe that you deserve respect? Do you demand respect? Why or why not?

_____

_____

_____

_____

_____

_____

_____

_____

_____

_____

_____

Have you discovered your special talents, skills, and abilities? If so, what are they?

_____

_____

_____

_____

_____

_____

_____

_____

_____

_____

What actions have you taken or should you be taking to further develop your special talents, skills, and abilities?

_____

_____

_____

_____

_____

_____

_____

_____

_____

_____

_____

Does your current occupation, training, or education relate to your special talents, skills, and abilities? If yes, how so?

_____

_____

_____

_____

_____

_____

_____

_____

_____

_____
_____
_____
_____
_____
_____
_____

You and only you
must determine your self-worth.

In what ways have you already taken action to empower yourself, or what further action will you take? Please be specific.

_____

_____

_____

_____

_____

_____

_____

_____

_____

_____

_____

_____

_____

_____

_____

_____

_____

_____

_____

_____

_____

_____

Questions invite answers, and answers invoke success.

I know I've asked you a lot of questions in this book. Probably more than most readers would prefer. But asking yourself questions and actually answering them, or at least making an attempt to, will bring you greater awareness. As you further investigate yourself for these vital answers, your revelations will become more and more significant.

If you don't know what you are worth, then you don't know what you are truly capable of accomplishing. It's impossible to tap into your ultimate potential when you place a low value on your self-worth.

Let me share with you one of my life experiences which taught me the value of self-worth.

This happened a little more than ten years ago, before I became a millionaire. I was down to my last $500 and rent, the car note, the kids' tuition, and every other bill was due. I couldn't get a loan from the bank because my credit was shot to the curb.

During this time, I got a phone call from a major record label. They wanted me to fly out to their headquarters in New York to meet with the president of their company. I had finally gotten an offer on the table (*a record deal*); it was the only offer, and it was going to change my life.

My brother and I flew to New York with airline

tickets paid for by the record company. As soon as we got to the office, we received the red carpet treatment. They said they were going to make us very rich men and fly us back home on their private jet once the deal was done. They even said that I didn't need a lawyer because this was going to be the best deal ever.

They offered to give me $1 million up front. My brother was anxiously telling me to sign—this was going to turn us into millionaires! I kept thinking to myself that it was the best thing that could ever happen to me. The president of the company gave me the contract, told me to take my time, read over it, and sign.

He pulled out a bottle of Cristal champagne, poured my brother and me a glass, and told me that this was only the beginning. There I was in the luxurious presidential office suite, sitting in the big, comfy leather chair, surrounded by marble floors and futuristic walls made of glass and mirrors. I was looking in the mirror, saying to myself, "The world is mine; I'm rich!" I was also looking at the contract and thinking that nothing else mattered but the million dollars.

For some reason, the fine print caught my eye . . . *seven-year deal . . . no other guaranteed monies . . . no rights to use my name ever again for the rest of my life!* I was selling my name and my brand, *Master P* and *No Limit Records*, FOR LIFE. I wouldn't be able to record with any other artist unless the company approved of it. They would own any product or music that I put out. Basically, I would be selling my soul for a million dollars.

When the president of the company left the room, I asked my brother why he thought this was such a great deal. He said, "ONE MILLION DOLLARS!" Neither of us had ever seen a million dollars. We just knew that this was going to change our lives. We were both so excited. And I knew I wasn't going to be able to leave that office without signing the contract. So I said to my brother, "Before I sign this, let's go to lunch and eat like millionaires."

I took him to a fancy restaurant where we spent about $200, and now I was down to my last $300. I called the president of the company, told him that I was going to let my lawyer look at the contract and that we'd be ready to sign tomorrow. I faxed the contract to my attorney, and he told me that it was the worst deal I would ever make in my life, but that the up-front money was probably more than I'd ever make in my life. So I had to make the decision: sell my soul or wait for another opportunity.

I decided to fly back home with my last $300. My brother sat on the plane next to me, disappointed and frustrated. We could have been rich. Instead, we were in the back of the plane, sitting in coach. We could have been flying back home on that private jet, picking out houses and cars in the morning.

Never make decisions out of desperation.

The more I thought about it, the more excited I became. I smiled to myself, thinking, *Here I am, from the ghetto, and this president of the music company doesn't even know me. But he was willing to give me a million dollars for my talent.*

And I started thinking, asking myself, *How talented am I? If he's offering me a million dollars, what am I really worth?*

When I got back home, I went straight to the studio and started making more music and thinking about how to improve myself so that maybe I would be offered $5 million next time. Well, a whole year went by without any other offers. But I was so confident in my product that I continued to sell it out of the trunk of my car and my business continued to grow. Instead of being an employee, I mastered the game of entrepreneurship. I sold over 200,000 units out of the trunk of my car.

Three months later, I was offered a record deal and a distribution deal by a major record company in California. They offered me $5 million up front for seven years, or 85 percent of every one of my records sold and no up-front money! With the 85 percent distribution deal, I would have to pay my own marketing budget; it would cost $200,000 to promote the record on a national level.

I chose the distribution deal. And I used the profits that I made from selling out of the trunk of my car to pay for the marketing costs. I had been getting ready to buy a house, but I had to put that dream on hold. Initially, my family was concerned, but they supported me. I thought to myself, *What do I have to lose? ... I came from nothing ... if I lose it all, I can start all over again.*

Six months later, I had sold over a million records, which profited me about $8 a record. So I bought an even bigger house than I had planned.

And 74 million records later, I was worth more than $400 million!

My grandfather always told me:

**"There's no limit to your self-worth;
your self-worth is priceless."**

I thank God that my self-worth was intact. I can't stress enough how important it is to **know** yourself and to **believe** in yourself even when it seems that no one else believes in you. Remember to take your time to think things through. You need to place a high value on your self-worth. It's good to heed people's advice if it's someone you trust, but it's wise to also weigh your own options and decide *for yourself* what's best for you. You create your own blueprint based on the value of your self-worth.

My thoughts, my ideas, my questions, my answers, my affirmations, and my revelations for *Chapter 6: What is the BLUEPRINT for Your SUCCESS?*

_____

_____

_____

_____

_____

_____

_____

_____

_____

_____

_____

_____

_____

_____

_____

_____

_____

_____

_____

_____

_____

_____

_____

_____

Chapter Seven

Guarantee Your SUCCESS by TAKING ACTION NOW

You have taken the initial step toward success by arming yourself with knowledge and awareness. Now it's time to make a plan and put it into action! Here's what you've accomplished so far:

☐ You have identified the stage of life that you are in:
Survival >>> Significance >>> Purpose

☐ You have a clear definition of what success is because you have defined it for yourself.

☐ You are cognizant of the fact that you are able to use your motivation to awaken your passion and create success.

☐ You understand the **7 Attitudes of Success** and know what types of attitudes attract success and distract you from success.

☐ You are aware of the **7 Hindrances to Success**, their various disguises, and how to overcome them.

☐ You are aware of the powerful effect the **7 Influential Factors to Self-Worth** have on your unique blueprint for success.

Now it's time to incorporate all that you have learned from this book and create the blueprint for your future successes in your personal life and/or in your business.

Remember that the choices you make or don't make today will determine your success or lack of it tomorrow. If you're not satisfied with *your* current life situation, it is your responsibility to make the necessary changes to achieve the results that you truly desire.

Plan of action

PART 1: Write Down Your Goal

Write your **short-term goal** (*up to 1 year*) in the <u>present tense</u>.

See the list of short-term goal examples.

- Be <u>specific</u> and realistic.

- State your <u>completion date</u> (month and year).

_____

_____

_____

_____

_____

_____

_____

_____

_____

_____

_____

_____

Examples of a <u>Short-Term Goal</u>:
Keep in mind that these are only examples. Every person has his or her own unique circumstances and capabilities. It may take you more or less time to accomplish certain goals. Remember, some of your short-term goals should relate to your long-term goals.

——— I weigh 30 pounds less by September 2007
(within six months)

——— I purchase my own business by March 2008
(within one year)

——— I repair my credit by March 2008
(within one year)

——— I am back in school by September 2007
(within six months)

——— I purchase my new car by September 2007
(within six months)

——— I establish a savings / investment account
by June 2007
(within three months)

You plan to fail when you fail to plan!

- Write your **long-term goal** (*up to 5 years*) in the <u>present tense</u>.

- Be specific and realistic.

- State your completion date (month and year).

_____

_____

_____

_____

_____

_____

_____

_____

_____

_____

_____

_____

_____

_____

_____

_____

_____

_____

Examples of a <u>Long-Term Goal</u>:

——— I earn my master's degree in business by March 2012 (within 5 years)

——— I make my real estate investment into a $1 million apartment building by March 2010 (within 3 years)

——— I make a down payment for my new five-bedroom home in the Westwood Estates by March 2012 (within 5 years)

——— I pay off all of my credit card debts by March 2012 (within 5 years)

PART 2: Write Down the Steps Necessary to Reach Your Goal

KNOWLEDGE. Knowledge, knowledge, and more knowledge is critical for success. You gain knowledge by educating yourself through your own committed research. It is your responsibility to educate yourself!

Gather all pertinent information that relates to your specific goal.

——— How much will it cost?

——— How long will it take?

——— What requirements need to be met?

——— What permits are needed?

——— Read everything that's available to you. The Internet, libraries, and bookstores are excellent resources.

Contact professionals and experts who are knowledgeable in the field that relates to your goal.

☐ Accountants

☐ Real Estate Agents

☐ Bankers

☐ Attorneys

☐ Financial Advisors

☐ Professors

☐ Family members and/or neighbors in the field related to your goal

Implement the time needed in your schedule of planning.

☐ If applicable, research where you can obtain the training and/or experience necessary to reach your goal.

☐ Organize your time. Set aside specific times and days on your calendar to invest your time and energy gaining knowledge, awareness, experience, training, education, etc. toward your goals. Be committed.

Don't allow distractions (people or things) to hinder your success.

There are no quick fixes and definitely no overnight success strategies. I can't stress enough the importance of planning. These are only general guidelines. Only *you* can actually create the proper blueprint to achieve your particular goal with your own exclusive plan.

However, I can share with you some simple strategic planning that I have used and found to be effective. And if you so choose, you can use it to help guide you as you set up your own personal plan of action toward success.

Every plan of action requires a personally customized blueprint to accommodate each individual and their circumstances. Each person's outcome will be different. It is important not to deviate from your plan; stick with it and ride it out. If necessary, find another route, research other options, but *never give up* on your dreams!

You must first perceive it before you can achieve it.

My desired goal was to be successful in the entertainment industry as an artist, entertainer, and an entrepreneur. In order for me to become a successful artist, entertainer, and entrepreneur, I had to first figure out how to please the consumers. I had to find out what attracted the consumers to buy what they were buying. And that's when I came up with my idea to open a record store.

Opening the record store was my short-term goal that would lead me to my long-term goal. This was the best way I could learn how to meet the specific needs of consumers. **Here is the plan of action that I incorporated to achieve my goal.**

Step #1: Knowledge

Knowledge truly is power. I went to the local library and researched every aspect of owning and running a record store. I also thoroughly researched the suppliers and distributors for the products I was going to be selling.

I took the time to read every book that I could get my hands on pertaining to the record store business. The Internet was not available to me at the time, so you know that I was determined because I invested forty consecutive days into the researching phase alone. Some people may not like to read, but if you want your business to be successful, you must arm yourself with knowledge.

Knowledge will protect you and help prevent avoidable, unnecessary mistakes.

Step #2: Training and Experience

I actually dove right into hands-on training and experience when I started my record store. Don't be afraid to make mistakes; when you learn from them, you gain experience and create success. Remember,

I mentioned earlier that everyone is different, situations and resources vary. Therefore, each person's successful plan of action toward reaching their goals will not be exactly the same. Remain committed to your blueprint for success.

Your success can only be as big as your vision.

Step #3: Naming My Business

Remember earlier in the book when I stated that words have creative power? Well, it's true. Take mine, for instance: *No Limit Records.*

I always knew that whatever I got into, there was going to be no limit to it—no limit to how much money I make, and no limit to the level of success that I achieve. So you've got to choose a business name that suits you and sets you up for greater success. If your vision is big, your success will be big.

If your dreams are big,
your expectations must be BIG.

Step #4: Selecting a Location with "No Limit" Potential

Find a location appealing to your purpose. In other words, make sure that there is a demand for the products and/or services that your business has to offer. For example, if you want to open up an athlete's shoe store, then it would be wise not to open up shop next to a Foot Locker, Finish Line, and the like.

The greater the need or demand that your business has to offer, the greater the potential your business has to grow. I had to scout out the best location for my record store and make sure there were no other businesses there that sold records.

Six weeks after I began my search, I discovered the ideal location. My first attempt was to work with a real estate agent, but I still couldn't afford the property that I desired. So I sought out the private owner and made an offer to fix up the property in exchange for six months of free rent. You need to be creative when it comes to resources and money.

Creativity is priceless;
it produces resources and income.

Step #5: Creative Marketing

Uniqueness and individuality are essential marketing tools for a successful business. Three months after finding the location for my record store, I opened up shop and printed up Grand Opening fliers and posted them everywhere, starting with the immediate area, the local neighborhood stores, barbershops, nail shops, and the nearest shopping malls.

I made sure that my prices were competitive in comparison to prices at the mall. I offered two-for-one deals. I came up with the idea to sell and rent out movies to make my record store even more special. I even sold toys, T-shirts, and hats to meet the demands of my consumers.

I also set up a system with FedEx and UPS. My customers could receive music the next day from other cities if I didn't have it available at my store that day. My motto was that I never turned down a customer: If I don't have it today, I will have it tomorrow. I sold a variety of music for consumers of all ages and all types: rap, R&B, country, gospel, you name it. I dealt with distributors nationwide.

Success increases
when creativity expands.

And to ensure visibility in my marketplace, I painted the entire building lime green to stand out above the rest. I wanted my record store to be noticeable.

Step #6: Building Successful Relationships

I became a part of the community by joining forces with the chamber of commerce, the local newspaper, and the radio station. I gained the community's respect and support by giving back to the people. I gave away free goods, free music, free T-shirts, etc. As I mentioned previously, I built such a good rapport with FedEx and UPS, I could guarantee my customers next day delivery on special orders.

Support those who support you;
it creates more power within your circle of
support.

It's important to build strong relationships with people who work for you, with you, and alongside you.

Step #7: Work Ethic

This is a step many businesses overlook, especially small businesses. Having the proper work ethic is vital to your business because the success of your business depends on it. Practice proper time management; being on time is important. Be considerate and respectful toward others because you want the same in return.

> *A successful entrepreneur has already established proper work ethics before starting his or her own business.*

For instance, if you advertise that your business opens at 9 a.m., be there early enough to be prepared to open promptly. Organization is essential. You want to have an efficient system set up from the start—one that includes preparing to open for business at the start of the day, running the business during operating hours, anticipating busy periods, and closing the business at the end of each day.

*"A true soldier always prepares for
war in a time of peace."*

I mentioned in a previous chapter that this is what my grandfather always told me. I applied this saying to my business. I choose to stay a step ahead of whatever I get involved in. The truth is that all businesses have their seasons; you have to be prepared for that.

And one other important thing to remember about a successful work ethic is that you should love to do what you do.

*Enthusiasm infused with passion
guarantees successful work ethics that last.*

Whatever business you venture into, you have got to invest some time into improving yourself and your business. Successful entrepreneurs are constantly thinking about how to promote their businesses, how to further benefit their consumers, how to increase profits, and how to minimize expenses.

Here are just a few more beliefs that I have put into practice and truly consider to be indispensable:

☐ Invest your money back into yourself / your business and forego luxury items until a later date.

☐ Take control of your finances. Know where your money is being spent—every dollar.

☐ Make working smart (not hard) a habit.

☐ Give back, tithe, and help others.

Success comes in progressive installments. Therefore, continuous self-improvement guarantees success. Now is the time to create your plan, work it, and *never give up!*

The truth is:
You have a choice to make.

Here's the last set of self-assessment questions in this book. Answering them will help you realize how close or far you are from reaching your goals.

This is serious business; it's important to be honest with yourself because your successful future is being birthed as you complete this chapter. The purpose of answering each question listed is to ensure that you are completely aware of your every-day life choices.

To be successful,
you must live each day to your fullest potential.

How are you spending your time? Are you in-vesting it or wasting it?

_____
_____
_____
_____
_____
_____
_____
_____
_____

Is your time organized? Do you have a writ-ten schedule?

_____
_____
_____
_____
_____
_____
_____

_____

_____

_____

_____

Do you have a written plan or a checklist of what you must accomplish every single day?

_____

_____

_____

_____

_____

_____

_____

What kinds of books are you reading, or tapes and CDs are you listening to? Are they related to your goals?

_____

_____

_____

_____

_____

_____

_____

_____

What kind of movies and television programs are you watching? How much of your time do you spend watching them, and are they related to your goals?

_____
_____
_____
_____
_____
_____
_____
_____
_____
_____

What do you do in your leisure time? What are your hobbies, and are they relevant to your goals?

_____
_____
_____
_____
_____
_____
_____
_____
_____

Are your goals moral, ethical, and legal?

_____
_____
_____
_____
_____
_____
_____
_____

Will anyone else benefit from your goals besides yourself?

_____
_____
_____
_____
_____
_____
_____
_____

Are you constantly looking for ways to improve yourself?

_____
_____
_____

_____

_____

_____

_____

How much time do you spend increasing your knowledge in the areas related to your goals?

_____

_____

_____

_____

_____

_____

_____

How much time do you spend researching information pertaining to your goals?

_____

_____

_____

_____

_____

_____

_____

What kind of people are you spending your time with? Are they "Dream Killers" or are they goal-driven?

_____

_____

_____

_____

_____

_____

_____

Are you taking care of your whole self—mind, body, and spirit?

_____

_____

_____

_____

_____

_____

Are you living a healthy, balanced lifestyle so that you can live long enough to reach your goals and fulfill your purpose in life?

_____

_____

_____

_____

_____

_____

Are you getting enough rest?

_____

_____

_____

_____

_____

_____

Are you exercising regularly?

_____

_____

_____

_____

_____

Are you eating healthily? What are you putting into your body?

_____

_____

_____

_____

_____

How are you spending your money?

_____
_____
_____
_____

How much of your finances have you invested toward your goal?

_____
_____
_____
_____
_____
_____
_____

Do you take your profits and splurge on luxury items, or do you reinvest it into your business and/or goals?

_____
_____
_____
_____
_____
_____
_____

Do you have a positive self-image and is your attitude toward life positive?

_____
_____
_____
_____
_____
_____

What is the legacy you plan on leaving behind?

_____
_____
_____
_____
_____
_____
_____
_____
_____

How will people remember you, especially your loved ones?

_____
_____
_____
_____

_____

_____

What type of attitudes are you passing on to your loved ones?

_____

_____

_____

_____

_____

_____

_____

_____

What thought and behavior patterns do you want your loved ones to inherit?

_____

_____

_____

_____

_____

_____

_____

_____

_____

_____

Now that you've taken the time to answer these questions truthfully, you are well aware of what changes need to be made in order to reach your highest level of success, discover your maximum potential, and fulfill your true purpose in life.

What will you do with your knowledge?

_____
_____
_____
_____
_____
_____

Knowledge does not guarantee success; it's what you do with your knowledge that creates change.

My thoughts, my ideas, my questions, my answers, my affirmations, and my revelations for *Chapter 7: Guarantee Your SUCCESS by TAKING ACTION NOW!*

_____

_____

_____

_____

_____

_____

_____

_____

_____

_____

_____

_____

_____

_____

_____

_____

_____

_____

_____

_____

_____

Conclusion

I'm living proof that success is guaranteed when you're committed to it. I came from an environment of poverty, lawlessness, defeat, deception, violence, fear, and extreme lack. But I overcame it. And you can do the same, no matter what your obstacles are.

You can use the talents and abilities that God has already given you instead of wasting time and energy wishing you were somebody else. You can begin to lay the foundation for building **Generational Wealth**.

My definition of **Generational Wealth** is the abundance of well-being and prosperity; it's so plentiful that it cannot be used up in one lifetime; it must be handed down from one generation to the next. **Well-Being** and **Prosperity** consist of the following:

- Wisdom = using your knowledge to create success

- Joy = spiritual elevation

- Happiness = contentment, pleasure, satisfaction, enthusiasm

- Security = freedom from worry and fear

- Positive Attitude = healthy thoughts and behavioral patterns

- Success = significant achievements that benefit others

- Great Wealth = a multiplicity in riches and in value of assets

Building Generational Wealth takes team effort.

You must establish successful relationships with your loved ones as well as business associates whose goals are related to yours. When teammates are committed to supporting one another, building each other up and not tearing each other down, you end up with a strong circle of support that will enable you to withstand the inevitable.

No one achieves success alone. For example, no one earns a degree solely through their own efforts. There are key players who have assisted and supported the graduate in some shape or form—whether those key players were parents, grandparents, siblings, friends, professors, tutors, or classmates.

Surround yourself with people who tell you, "You can do it!" rather than "You can't . . ." Distance yourself from **"Dream Killers," "Crabs in a Bucket,"** and people who **Complain, Compare,** and **Covet**. Reach out to people who are smarter than you and show you how *you can!*

Knowledge is more valuable than money.

With knowledge, you create income. Money is a tool. Don't be a slave to it. Don't work for money; make money and use it to create a cash flow so that your money works for you. Do your research. Use your talents, abilities, and desires for the benefit of others. Discover your true purpose and success will follow. It's never too early or too late to build **Generational Wealth**. Your loved ones are witnessing and inheriting your attitudes, your thoughts, your actions, and your successes. Each day, you're setting the standard for your own success.

I would like to take this opportunity to thank you for allowing me to share some of my personal and business related experiences with you. And finally, I'd like to share one more of my truths with you: I've found that true success is not possible unless I have God in my life.

"And you shall remember the Lord your God, for it is He who gives you power to get wealth . . ." —**Deuteronomy 8:18**

God gives each of us the ability to become rich, and when we allow and ask Him to move in our lives, sorrow does not accompany our riches. When you make things happen without God, attaining and maintaining success eventually wears you out and tears you down.

> *"The blessing of the Lord, it maketh rich,*
> *and He added no sorrow with it."*
> *—Proverbs 10:22*

Notes

_____

_____

_____

_____

_____

_____

_____

_____

_____

_____

_____

_____

_____

_____

_____

_____

_____

_____

_____

_____

_____

_____

_____

_____

AFTERWORD

There are no coincidences in life when you trust God each day as you actively seek out to reach your goals. His Divine favor will order your steps into your purposeful destiny . . . if you never give up!

My son, Romeo, and I were exploring the possibility of him attending a university in the Bay Area. I vividly remember having a conversation with Magic Johnson and his colleagues about this. And they mentioned that if I was thinking of buying a home in San Francisco, they highly recommended this sharp real estate guy that they had recently met named Curtis Oakes. So I called Curtis immediately to set up an appointment so that he could show me some houses. Curtis and I got together on an early Saturday morning and right away we clicked! Through our conversations we discovered how much we have in common, although we live very different lives.

When Curtis told me that he did more than just sell real estate; that he had worked with Robert Kiyosaki, the author of *Rich Dad Poor Dad*, and that he also authored two CD's with Donald Trump called the *Three*

Master Secrets of Real Estate Success, and *Bubble Proof Real Estate Investing*, I was impressed! During this time in my life, I was already in the mode of doing my own research on making wise financial investments through real estate properties using the money that I've profited from the Hip Hop industry and filmmaking. Curtis was the missing piece to the puzzle for me stepping up my game in the real estate business.

Only a few days later, I flew to Scottsdale, Arizona to meet Robert Kiyosaki and sat in on two of his teaching sessions. I also attended The Wealth Expo in New York with Donald Trump and Robert Kiyosaki. Curtis exposed me to a whole new world. I learned how to take my already successful business to a higher level of success! I discovered how to raise money for my business ventures through Wall Street. With my newly found knowledge, I became excited about the transition that was taking place in my career and consequently the evolution in my life.

I knew that it could only be through God that we met, we come from two completely different worlds! What are the chances of me meeting someone that could educate me about real estate, help launch my book, *Guaranteed Success*, and partner up with me to do the very thing that God put on my heart; to encourage people, to change their vision of their future and to have big dreams and goals, focusing on knowledge not money, and to build generational wealth, (not generational poverty).

I was searching for a way to get God's will done. Curtis had been working on encouraging people for years through his work with Robert Kiyosaki and Donald Trump, with little success in the African American Community. Curtis had told me that the day before I called him he was frustrated with speaking at events for so many years only to find a small percentage of people getting his message. Curtis felt as though he had to make a decision to stop teaching, and go back to just focusing on being a real estate broker, developer and investor until he met me. Curtis taught me the real estate and finance game and I taught him how to take a stand; believe in your entrepreneurship skills and independently make your business-related visions come to life.

Nonetheless, in 2006 our destinies intertwined. During our telephone conversations we talked for hours about having similar backgrounds; growing up in the ghetto; our desire to bring up the next generation of American youth to give them a chance to make it in life, and how we wanted to change the world! Thus, the Miller Oakes Financial Learning Center was born.

I saw in Curtis Oakes a guy who had an enormous amount of knowledge in the areas of real estate and finance. I signed up for his real estate mentoring program so that he could personally mentor me. I believe that our collective efforts can change the way people think about their situations. His diligence has led him to what I believe is his destiny. I also believe that my diligence in wanting to build generational wealth led me to my destiny as well. **Applied Knowledge is Power!**